Wilderness Reflections

Table of Contents

By Michael J Bullard

Introduction – Wilderness Reflections

If you were my son or daughter and I could take you hunting, fishing, canoeing and camping with me, this book represents what I would want you to know about the outdoors that I have come to love. How to hunt, fish, canoe and camp is important and there are many tips and techniques presented in this book to help you succeed with these endeavors. However, the ultimate goal of these outdoor activities is to fully comprehend and appreciate the wilderness around you and your relationship to it. I have thrown in a few life lessons that experience has taught me are important also. Many of the tips and techniques will be related to you through stories that come from 50 years of wandering in the woods and fields, lakes and streams of Iowa while hunting, fishing, camping, scouting and running my dogs.

In our fast paced world with all the responsibilities and multi-tasking it takes to get through a typical day, we don't get nearly enough time to simply sit and reflect on what is important to us. Most people do not realize what they are missing because they have never had the luxury of time to themselves. I am not talking about the few hours here and there while waiting for a soccer game to get over or while waiting for a plane to arrive. I am talking about a few days alone with nothing to do but hike or canoe until it is time to set up the next camp and make the next meal. Time enough to think deeply and reflect on accomplishing the plans God has for your life.

Because we are made in God's image and God is spirit, there is a spiritual side to life that takes some time and contemplation to become aware of. Immersing yourself in nature via the American wilderness is a tremendous way to reflect and get in touch with nature and your spiritual side. I make no apology for relating insights about the spiritual side of life because all creation testifies that there is a creator God. Don't dismiss this idea without a thorough investigation. You will be held accountable for what you know or should have known about God because of the wonders of the natural world around you. I have seen and experienced things that leave me no doubt that there is a God in heaven that loves you very much. God has a plan for your life, a plan to prosper you and not to harm you. But God is a gentleman; he will not come into your life until you invite him in. After that you will enjoy a close fellowship with Him and He will bless your life.

March

March is often called the starving month for nature's creatures. Every year in Iowa, we plant millions of acres of corn and soybeans then in the fall we harvest them. In the 1960's, the harvest left a lot of weedy picked cornfields with a lot of spilled corn resting undisturbed until the spring plowing season. The pheasants had a lot of food for the winter in the 1960's. Today, farmers have become much more efficient in getting the maximum harvest from their farm acres. The combines now leave little spilled corn. Some farmers turn their cattle out into the fields to clean up what little corn can be found along with the stalks. Almost all the farmers now use fall plowing to increase their yields. The soil is so compacted from overuse that they have found plowing in the fall will help to decompose the corn stalks over the winter so that the ground will be less compacted in the spring when they plant the new crop. Fall plowing leaves no food for the pheasants and deer. Farming is big business in Iowa and in order for farmers to pay for their land and expensive machinery, the pressure is on to farm fence row to fence row and to utilize fall plowing to increase yields because everyone else is doing it.

In the 60's there were few deer in Iowa because of overharvesting. Now, the deer are abundant because of better game management practices by the Department of Natural Resources (DNR). Every year the deer have plenty of food to help them raise their new family but come winter, much of the food is removed with today's efficient farming practices. Without hunting pressure to remove some of the deer there would be more starvation than there already is.

4

Similarly, songbirds have little to eat in March after the fall food supply has been eaten and buried under the snow all winter. I think birds prefer to find their own food when they can. I feed them at my feeder through March but then I do not see them as often in April when new food springs forth from the earth.

Animals work hard during the winter to find adequate food supplies. I fed some pheasants during the winter and when the snow became deep, I was surprised to see them sitting in my ninebark bushes eating the seed clusters above the snow. Turkeys roam the forests of Iowa in the winter time scratching through the snow and turning up leaves everywhere to find some acorns buried under the snow. Deer will browse the juniper trees when the snow gets deep. They do not eat them at other times of the year so I think they are not as well-liked as other plants but they will do in a pinch. Rabbits eat the bark of the small trees higher and higher as the snow piles deeper and deeper. Finding the saplings in the spring with the bark stripped up to 2 or 2 ½ feet tall leaves one wondering how big those rabbits were! The answer is really how deep the snow that the rabbits were sitting on was.

I like a cup of plain black tea in the afternoon to remind me of the woods. Frederic Leopold, the brother of the famous Conservationist Aldo Leopold once told me "Tea is the woodman's drink" when we enjoyed a cup of tea after a winter walk in the woods. Tea is light to carry and easily brewed over a fire which is why it is the "Woodsman's" drink he explained. I enjoy remembering walks with Frederic and his wife Edith. Edith could tell me all the different kinds of mouse tracks in the snow. Frederic showed me how to identify trees in the winter time. Just being exposed to those ideas was enough to get me thinking. So, a cup of tea makes me think of the woods and campfires past. I use it to slow myself down and reflect.

This last fall, I got into my tree stand very early before sunrise and could hear little tiny noises in the leaves on the forest floor. They sounded a bit like squirrels but it was too early for squirrels to be up and the noises were too faint. It turns out they were woodland voles and they disappeared into a dead tree as soon as the first light from the sunrise started to show. I think Edith would be pleased at my discovery of woodland voles in the forest.

March is still a very good time to scout for deer and listen for turkeys. You may even find some shed antlers or deer skulls from ones that were never recovered. The deer trails really stand out in March as all the leaves have decomposed and the trails stand barren and black in the forest before the understory starts greening up. I like to look for trails coming out of the timber and going into farmland where there is a narrow section of trees projecting out into the alfalfa and corn fields. These can be good areas in the morning as deer come back into the main woods to sleep and spend their day after carousing and feeding all night.

We like to get out into the woods before sunup in late March and listen as the turkeys fly down from their roosts and gobble. You can make a great horned owl call and get the turkeys to gobble nervously and disclose their location when they are still roosted in the trees.

April

In April the earth wakes up again. Trees start to bud out with the softer trees like maple leading the way and harder trees like oak sleeping in. Can you identify the types of trees in the winter before they have their leaves on? You need to look at both the bark and the structure and symmetry of the branches in order to do so. A thorough investigation of the forest floor for old leaves and nuts might help to confirm your hypothesis.

Many years ago I was lucky enough to find a magic fishing hole. It was at a sandpit. I was fishing with a fly rod and I could cast to a spot about the size of a garbage can lid and the crappies were just boiling the water there. Many times they would jump clear out of the water and hit my popper on the way down. That is a pretty ferocious bite in anyone's book. I landed 54 crappies in about 30 minutes. I did not take time to put them on the stringer; I just unhooked them and let them flop in the spring grass. It took a lot longer to clean them than it did for me to catch them!

I sometimes buy a Turkey license in the spring. Mostly because I have a friend that really enjoys turkey hunting. Last April I did not get a turkey but I had a wonderful time sitting on a hilltop in the woods. The hilltop was covered in wild geranium blossoms. It was windy and cold so I was huddled up with my back to a tree trying to stay warm as it started to snow. As the sun brightened the sky, the snow started picking up steam, driven by the wind. The snow soon started covering the fallen trees and sticking to the wild geranium plants. My hunt was cut short by a minor family emergency but I still enjoy remembering the experience of the early spring snowstorm in the woods.

Some of the earliest plants you will see in the woods are the wild geraniums, trillium, may-apple, jack in the pulpit and of course the elusive and highly sought after morel mushroom. There is a large group of people of Czechoslovakian decent in my home town and every spring they have a Houby days festival to celebrate the morel mushroom. Fried in butter then whipped into an omelet, morel mushrooms taste exquisite. About the time that the may apples bloom, the first dandelions appear and the apple trees bloom is the time to go mushroom hunting. People will tell you that the first 70 degree days will cause the mushrooms to start growing. If you find a patch of mushrooms, you would be wise to keep their location to yourself. At $20 per pound and with their delectable flavor, they are quite a temptation to interlopers. My friend says that he puts a lock on his deer stand in the woods, "To keep the honest people honest".

Integrity is measured by how you act when no one else is around. I like to think that integrity is measured by the little things. Maybe you would never steal but if you discover that the clerk gave you an extra dollar in change, is your integrity important enough for you to return it? I tell my kids that you can judge a person's true character by how they react in a stressful situation. If someone just destroyed your property or somehow violated your "rights" do you react with anger seeking retribution or are you self controlled enough to react with patience and understanding? If someone makes fun of another person and says unkind things about them under stress, you should be cautious of that person because that reflects their true character.

Over the winter, the process of freezing and thawing has caused the seeds sown in the fall to work their way into the soil. It has also stratified some of them so that the hard outer shell is sufficiently deteriorated to allow the seeds to start growing in the spring. I have about 1,000 square feet of perennial prairie flowers and grasses in my yard. In April, the small plants just break through the soil with their tiny first leaves to make a carpet of tiny green leaves. I really enjoy my prairie plants as they seem to have a zest for life. They spring forth with great strength every year and stand up to whatever the weather might throw at them. A major drought is only a temporary set back to my prairie plants. They never seem to fall victim to any mold or blight that my hybridized varieties seem to fall victim to every year. They bear an abundance of seeds which the song birds enjoy.

In the Bible it says we humans see spiritual things dimly as through a glass. Now, I am not a professional scientist but I have taken chemistry, physics, biology, botany and zoology at the college level and know a few things about scientific principles of our natural world. I certainly understand genetic mutation and can see how species evolve over time to develop certain traits. Most any scientist will tell you that when they alter the genetic traits of a plant to develop longer bloom time or heavier seed production, they usually get some other traits coming along as excess baggage. The susceptibility to mold and blight seem to be the major unwanted traits passed along to my hybridized varieties of flowers.

I have some blazing stars in my yard that I bought from Earl May garden center. Every year they bloom profusely and I have to cut off the seed heads as there are so many. I have only one Rough Blazing Star plant in my yard. It is a native prairie plant and blooms at the same time as the Earl May blazing stars. What is so weird to me is that the one native prairie blazing star will attract all the butterflies while the dozens of hybridized varieties sit butterfly-less. The color of the blooms seems the same to me. The hybridized varieties actually have more blooms along their stems but the butterflies prefer the native plant. The native prairie flower's nectar must be sweeter is my assumption. Jesus told us to "Consider the lilies of the field, they neither weave nor spin but not even Solomon was arrayed like one of these. If that is how God clothes the grass of the field that is here one day then thrown into the fire, how much more does He care for you, oh you or little faith?"

I live in Iowa and it is obvious what Pioneer and Dekalb and Asgrow have done with the genetic traits of corn and soybeans over the years. But my belief in evolution stops at the micro level. I do not believe in macro evolution explaining the creation of the universe and our world. I see too much complexity and order in the natural world to believe in macro evolution. Do you know how many chemical reactions occur in your nerve synapses in order for your brain to feel the pain from a pin prick or the heat from a match on your finger? Do you know the chemical reactions that take place in the ATP-ADP cycle to give your muscles energy from the food you eat and the oxygen that you breathe? Have you studied the simplicity and the complexity of the DNA molecule? Given the second law of thermodynamics; that left to itself everything tends towards disorder, I can't believe that the order I see in the world around me happened by chance.

Man has done wondrous things with genetic mutation and cloning but I believe that only God causes the spark of life to appear. Furthermore, I believe that God is both the creator and the sustainer of life on this world including both you and I and every living thing both plant an animal. Without God's sustaining hand, life would cease. Before you dismiss that theory as superstition, remember the Bible says we are dead to spiritual things until we are born again spiritually by God's grace through our faith which He gives us. Even after we are born again spiritually, we only see spiritual things dimly as through a glass. So, take the few things you do know about God and extrapolate them and then determine if the ever present creator and sustainer of life supporting life on this earth might be a possibility.

Anyway, that is what I think about when I look at my perennial flower beds and see the mass of little first leaves sprouting from the seeds that have hibernated over the winter....

One of my favorite activities in April is to go stand below dams and wing dams on the Wapsipinicon River when the sun is coming up and fish for walleyes and northern pike. The DNR has stocked walleye fingerlings into the Wapsi for many years. There are more fish per cubic acre of water in the Wapsi River than many of the lakes around here. The river is usually running fast in the spring and I prefer to fish from shore below dams where the fish seem to congregate rather than risk putting my canoe out into the fast cold water. I do however enjoy floating my canoe in some of the

11

local lakes and trying to catch some crappies. They are among the first fish to start getting active in the spring.

There are a few things about fishing that you should know…. The colder the water, the slower the retrieve you should use. Because fish are cold blooded, their metabolism is slow when the water is cold. A slow retrieve is more enticing or natural to them. Also, you should try to match the color of your lure to the clarity of the water. If the water is clear try to use white, or lime green or yellow. If the water is darker or you are fishing deeper, use darker colors like purple, brown or black. In the spring you can fish shallower. Fishing from the surface to 5 feet down is common. The fish will congregate in the warmer shallows in the spring. Fish only feel pain through their eyes and they have no eyelids so the brightness from the sun is a major factor in fishing for most species. When the sun is high and the water is clear and there is no chop on the water, the fish will be deep or hiding in the weeds. Fish relate to underwater structure. I once sat in a boat over a rocky underwater ridge that ran out into deep water up on to a rocky flat area on a clear northern lake straight lining black leeches in about 5 feet of water as the sun went down. The smallmouth bass were following that ridge up from the deep into the shallows to hunt for food as the sun went down. The fish finder told me that we may have been catching one out of every five fish that came under my boat. The action was fast as the big school of small mouth bass headed into the shallows. Fishing at sundown and into the early evening is sometimes necessary on these clear cold lakes in the north woods.

I have had a similar experience with large schools of rock bass that come into the reed beds following a particular point in the reeds that stretches out into deeper water. Using a long cane pole and a slip bobber and a leech, we were catching them as fast as we could unhook one and lower the leech down again as they moved into the reeds at sundown.

May

May is the gardening month in Iowa. By mid-May the chance of frost should be gone. Hopefully over the winter you have had enough time to plan your garden because this month you can stay busy tilling the soil and planting the garden. Planting a prairie is a long term adventure. The first year the seeds grow very little as they spend more energy establishing roots. That is why they recommend keeping them mowed from 4 to 6 inches the first year. That will keep the competitor weeds mowed down so they do not go to seed while the seedling prairie plants hang out under the blade. The second year, prairie plants will start to show more enthusiasm but you will still be wondering if planting them was a mistake. The third year, your doubts will be removed as the prairie plants show up with abandon. By the fifth year, there will be no stopping your prairie and you will wonder what you have started.

I have ordered seed from Prairie Nursery and Prairie Restorations, Inc. with good success in the past. They sell top quality native grass and flower seeds and plants and seed mixes. They both have a very informative website and a good online catalog. If you get the Prairie Nursery catalog, it makes a really good field identification guide to native plants. I have bought prairie mixes from other vendors and been disappointed. Some mixes have plants that I do not want such as common evening primrose and cupplant. They tend to take over the garden.

The reason I like gardening with prairie flowers so much is that they are tough perennial plants that need little attention. They support many kinds of insects, birds and butterflies. I enjoy the viewing and photographing opportunities they provide. Prairies are constantly changing. Every month it seems like new waves of color and textures take over. It is kind of like watching a parade as the processional of flowers marches their way over the landscape.

If your monetary investments yielded a return as bountiful as your investment in prairie seeds you would be rich beyond your wildest dreams. Prairie plants are vigorous with their deep root systems and prolific seed generation. Some may out-compete others but with a little planning you can mitigate that effect. For instance, I am currently planning a large prairie restoration project where I will have a short grass prairie in the front on the western edge and then a tall grass prairie to the east of the short grass and then a plot of switch grass farthest to the east. Since seeds generally spread by the wind and the wind typically blows from the west, by locating the taller and more vigorous grasses further downwind I am hoping to limit their intrusion into the short grass prairie.

In May, we have a tradition of camping the week before Memorial Day with some friends in the Yellow River Forest in northeast Iowa. It is great to be out in the newly greened up landscape after being cooped up in the house over the winter. Northeast Iowa is sometimes called little Switzerland. There are many small trout streams running between high bluffs. We like to camp the week before Memorial Day to get away from the Memorial Day crowds. The kids like wading in the cold creek and fishing for trout. I like to use the smallest Panther Martin spinners to catch trout in the Yellow River trout streams. I have also seen great success with floating wax worms on a trout hook down into their pools. I saw a kid cleaning up on trout using small crappie minnows once.

One technique I have seen used with great effectiveness is to get some extra line out in your non-rod holding hand and side-arm lob your hook out into the pool as you let the extra line shoot out through the rod guides. The extra line allows the hook to fall straight down into the pool as if no line is attached to it, like it fell unhindered from the sky. If you cast your hook without doing this, it immediately starts to sweep down stream because of the current pulling on the tight line. Using the extra line shooting out so that the bait falls straight down without imparting any action from the current seems to elicit a strike response from the trout. It may be because most of the trout in Iowa are hatchery raised trout and the trout food pellets fell like that in their rearing ponds. Anyway, I watched a young kid do that with great effectiveness in the pool I had been fishing with no luck one day and he was using a kernel of canned sweet corn!

I have watched trout in a pool get excited over my offering for a couple casts then ignore it. I tie on a new offering and they get excited again then ignore that one also. So be ready to tie on new lures, a small white twister tail, a

15

yellow marabou crappie jig, a panther martin spinner. I like catching them on top water insects so I can see the strike. Hopefully you are using a very light and limp monofilament. My science teacher friend that let me in on the wax worm secret weapon uses a light fluorocarbon leader which is essentially invisible to the sharp eyed trout. Also, the trout will be facing upstream so approach the pools from downstream, stay low and cast upstream as much as possible.

      We like to cook the fresh trout over the open campfire. I have watched enough new scouts try to start a fire that I will offer some quick advice here. You need to gather your tinder, tiny sticks, small sticks, medium sticks and larger sticks first before you strike the first match. Hopefully you will need only one match! If it is windy, you can make the small starter fire on the leeward side of some big logs to block the wind. Get a loose ball of tinder about the size of your fist made out of dry grass, dry weeds or crumpled up leaves. Leaves laying flat on each other do not offer enough air circulation for the flame to take off. You can then make a teepee of tiny dry sticks around and on top of the tinder ball. Leave a hole on the leeward side to put the match in. Hopefully you gathered your sticks from above the forest floor so they are really dry and not damp from laying on the ground. Build the teepee up with small and medium sized sticks over the tiny sticks. Remember heat rises so you want to build it tall to catch the heat. You can now light your fire at the base of the tinder. You may have to put some more dry grass or a few crumpled leaves and tiny sticks above your teepee to pull the flame up through your sticks before you add the larger sticks then a small log then some larger logs.

We like to put the trout in a flat hinged basket with long handles specifically designed to cook fish over a fire. You can simply roll the trout up in some heavy foil with some butter, spices and slices of onion or lemon and cook it right over or on the coals of the fire. Hopefully you brought a hot pad or a leather glove! It does not take long to cook the trout so the meat flakes off the bones easily.

One of my first memories as a child is fishing for trout in Swiss Valley up by Dubuque when I was about 4 years old. I was fishing with a cane pole and a night crawler when a big German Brown trout flashed quickly through the riffles to attack my bait then just about pulled the pole out of my little hands before he jumped high above the creek right in front of me, glinting in the sun as he threw the hook. What a beautiful fish! I was awestruck and I can still see that colorful fish shining in the sun 50 years later. If God lavishes that much beauty on a trout, how much more does he care for you who are made in his own image, a spiritual being?

June

The earliest prairie plants start to show up this month. Shooting stars and lance leaf coreopsis and Michigan lilies all are among the first to bloom in June. I enjoy watching the goldfinch eating my lance leaf coreopsis seed heads. They must be a preferred food source because they really flock to them.

You owe it to yourself to buy a fly rod and practice whipping the air in your yard until you can straighten the line out behind you and shoot it out straight in front of you. That is the dues you pay in order to participate in one of life's' greatest fishing adventures close to home. It happens in late May or early June around here. The bluegills move on to their spawning beds! There is nothing better than to slip quietly into the back of a sandy bay in your small boat and with polarized sunglasses, see the saucer shaped holes in the sandy shallows that promise fast action with aggressive bluegills. Bluegills are insectivores. When the male bluegills are on their beds they are also very territorial. If you cast a small popper above their beds, they will teach you why they are called poppers! They suck in the popper with a loud popping sucking sound. If you stick your finger in the side of your mouth inside your cheek and pop it out, you will hear the exact sound the aggressive little buggers make when they attack your popper. That sound is followed by the zip of your line across the water as you raise your pole tip to set the hook and then the fight is on. Mister bluegill turns his flat side to you and tries the end around play as he shakes his head against the tension of the line. The furious battle does not last long and to the victor comes the wonderful sight of big dark colored bluegill with its shiny dark blue tab on the gill plate and orange throat. The older I get the less I like cleaning fish so I throw him back after his out of water experience.

We like to go to Minnesota in June for summer vacations. We usually rent a cabin from one of the many resorts on one of the 1,000 lakes. I remember asking the owner of the resort if there was any underwater structure in the lake that was not on the published depth maps. He told me about a small underwater island about 150 yards from shore that reached up to about 10 feet of water. I triangulated it using his directions and my depth finder confirmed it rising from the deep. I anchored my boat on the main lake side of the island and straight-lined some big minnows under the boat. Wow what a fishing hole! I filled a stringer with 3 to 5 pound northern pike. At that size they put up a good fight. I still dream about going back to that underwater island and checking out the northern pike population.

On another, bigger underwater island in a Minnesota lake, I had a different experience. This island had more vegetation and it produced some big largemouth bass and northern pike. But, what I most remember about this island is the giant musky. I had a new deep diver lure that dives down 15 to 17 feet deep. I was throwing that lure around the base of the island where it started to rise from the deep. I was looking down into the water to see the lure as it came back to the boat when the sight of a musky bigger than my leg materialized behind my lure. My reaction was to pull the lure out of the water as it scared me to see that big musky only a few feet away with its teeth hanging out all of a sudden like that. His head seemed almost as big as a spade.

One of my favorite rigs for testing out new water because it will catch most everything is a simple Lindy rig with a egg sinker, bb split shot, orange float, #6 offset hook and a minnow, leech or night-crawler hooked through the nose. You may have to let the fish run with the minnow or especially the night-crawler before you set the hook after you feel the tap-tap of a hit. The line feeds out through the egg sinker easily as the fish runs with it so it feels no resistance and does not drop the bait. Letting the fish run with it can be a matter of simply lowering your rod tip for a second or, you can release the bail and let it spool off some line for 5 to 8 seconds. Keep count of the number of seconds and if you are not getting hook ups, increase the time you let the fish run with the bait. Little fish seem to give a quick tap-tap-tap and then zip off with the bait, maybe because other little fish are trying to steal it from them. Bigger fish sometimes just grab it and move off steadily. Let the line tighten up before you set the hook with a solid snap of the wrist and raise of the forearm. Remember you are setting the hook through the elasticity or stretch of the monofilament line so you need to send a good sharp wave of energy down the line to drive that hook into their bony mouth. Be sure to duck if the sinker flies up towards the boat!

You can fish the Lindy rig along a weed edge, where the weeds thin out because of lack of light penetration. You can fish on gravel or sand bars that rise out of the mud bottom. Remember fish relate to changes in structure on the bottom. You can hang a Lindy rig straight over the side of the boat. I sometimes fan cast over an area to explore it in an organized fashion. Throw a cast at 12 o'clock then the next cast at 1 o'clock then the next at 2 etc. until you have covered the entire area looking for fish in the most time efficient manner.

If you cover more water when looking for fish, you will increase your chances of catching them. Crank baits are an effective way to cover a lot of water. I like to use the crawdad colored crank baits with a rattle in them for small mouth bass. I like slow trolling a shad rap over the gravel flats in the early evening in about 5 or 6 feet of water for walleyes. I always like drifting across an underwater island or down across a point or down a weed line if the wind is not too strong. You can use your motor as a rudder to control the direction of your drift and your boat position against the wind. A lot of guys like to put the motor in reverse and back troll along the structure or break line where the bottom falls off, kind of like an underwater bluff. If you want to catch fish, you have to keep your line in the water!

I did not mention using a Johnson silver minnow with a pork rind frog in the reeds. It is weedless and catches a lot of bass and northern pike in the otherwise hard to fish reeds. I have a friend that does pretty well on largemouth bass in the spring using purple worms with a Texas rig, bullet weight and large worm hook.

July

In July the prairie flowers are really getting started. My ox eye sunflowers and spiderwort plants are always impressive. I like the spiderworts or rain lilies as they are sometimes called because they are open in the morning showing their blue or lavender blooms but if I come home for lunch, they are all closed up to the sun. The ox eye sunflowers have a beautiful shade of orange tinted yellow. They stand on strong stems and the gold finch love their oil rich seeds.

I have put my cup plants into detention. I have isolated them into their own little corner of the yard. They are an impressive plant but they tend to take over. They are a native sunflower that can reach up to 7 or 8 feet tall. Each stem can get up to 50, four inch wide yellow sunflowers. The stems are square the whole way up and the rough leaves are opposite each other and join to form a cup around the stem that can hold a substantial amount of water after a rain. I have seen birds and insects drinking from the cup of water. A certain type of beetle flocks to this plant to pollinate it. It spreads easily and forms a large colony. It is quite a bird seed producer and really brings in the goldfinches.

In July, the river levels start to fall. In Iowa it is legal to camp on the sandbars of "Meandering" streams. There is more life on the Wapsipinicon River than there is in the boundary waters and my old canoe is the only ticket necessary to participate in this adventure. My kids used to be scared of the raccoon noises at night on the sandbar. It could be because of the stories I used to tell them about the raccoons when they were little I suppose. We have fun wading for discarded clam shells or finding live clams. They say you can judge the health of a river by its clam population. The raccoon tracks along the shore tell me that the health of the river and its clam population is appreciated by the masked marauder. We also like to seine our own minnows and then bait bank poles and trot lines. It is exciting for the kids to see the different kinds of minnows that come up in the seine. Sometimes we salt them down in the sun to dry them out and toughen them up so they stay on the hook better. There is nothing better than waking up early on a sandbar and seeing your bank pole bending over, up and down against the current. It is so exciting to find out what you have hooked into overnight that is pulling so hard on your bank pole or trot line.

I still remember my young son and his friend checking a trot line. They were so excited to pull the heavy trot line up out of the muddy Cedar River until they saw what was on the other end. Their excitement turned to fear and they dropped the line when they saw the prehistoric monster on the other end. That must be what a big alligator snapping turtle looks like to a couple young kids! And to imagine you are wading in the same water with that beast! We usually cut the line and let him have the hook. The hook will disintegrate soon enough in the muddy water. Since then, I have learned how to clean a turtle the right way from some old salt that we met at a state park. It is still a lot of work however and I would only do it to teach a kid the proper technique. Your reward for the hard work is some exotic turtle soup. I have about a pound and a half in my freezer right now from last summers trot line adventure waiting to be turned into turtle soup.

Something else you will see along a river is an abundance of bird life. Common birds you will see in Iowa are kingfishers, little green herons, big blue herons and some wood ducks. In the winter you will see a lot of eagles along the river. On summer evenings you will see a lot of bats swooping above the water. It is memorable to be paddling back from setting out trot lines after dark and watching the bats swoop around you as a raccoon swims across in front of you and scampers across the muddy sand bar.

I can remember times spent wading up a small creek and seeing carp scooting away making a v in the water or surprising a big blue heron and seeing him take off out of the little creek. Generally the wood duck jump and fly away quite a ways off. It is hard to get real close to them. The kingfishers have a very distinctive call and they are not bashful about using it.

My friend that sells a lot of kayaks said that people do not buy as many canoes because they are harder to learn how to paddle. It does not take much practice to paddle a canoe. Getting into a canoe can be the hardest part! You have to always maintain three points of contact with the canoe when you are getting into it. That usually means that you have both hands on the gunwales balancing your weight as you crawl towards your seat. When you are seated, you can brace your knees against the sides to help stabilize the canoe. When solo canoeing or in a strong wind, you can kneel with your knees against the side to lower your center of gravity, balance your weight and give you more leverage to paddle. Paddling from the rear requires you to learn the J-stroke in order to paddle in a straight line. A J-stroke is simply a deep stroke parallel to the canoe but at the end of the stroke you turn the blade and push it out away from the canoe to counteract the action of your deep stroke. When you take a deep stoke at the back of the canoe on the right side for instance, you will force the front to the left. Pushing the paddle to the right, away from the canoe at the end of the stroke will cause the front of the canoe to kick back to the right counteracting the effect of your deep stroke.

If you have a strong paddler in front, their paddling on the left can counteract your paddling on the right so that you do not have to J-stroke as much. If you have a very strong paddler in the front, you can counteract them by leaning the canoe towards their side with your butt on the seat. If the canoe is slightly leaning to the side the front person is paddling on, they will have more difficulty overpowering your deep stroke in the back and you wont have to change sides paddling as often.

For quick maneuvering in tight spots paddling backwards in the back can really make the front of the canoe behave as you want it to. Sometimes the front paddler needs to paddle sideways or backwards in tricky maneuvers.

Solo paddling a canoe can be done by kneeling behind the thwart just behind the middle of the canoe for better control. You can also put a pack or water jug or bicycle in the front of the canoe for better weight distribution.

August

August is when the prairie flowers really come on strong. Ironweed, many sunflowers and coneflowers, butterfly milkweed and swamp milkweed are all blooming now. My Ironweed is aptly named for its strong stems. I think you could weave a strong rope from the fibers of its stem. I like to put some butterfly milkweed plants out by my mailbox so the people walking by can stop and wonder about the orange flower masses. I enjoy all the butterflies that it brings in as well. It seems like we usually get a 4 to 6 week drought every year around August. The ground gets as hard as a rock and large cracks form in the dirt. I rarely water my prairie flowers. They do not seem to wilt much under the heat and always bounce back with a little rain. Have you ever noticed that rain is much better for plants than tap water? I would say it is 3 or 4 times better for watering plants to use rain water. I imagine it is because the rain water falls down through the atmosphere picking up nitrogen along the way. I like to think of it as God caring for his flowers by watering them.

In August, it seems like I always make a last ditch effort to do something memorable before the summer slips away and school starts up again. A great trip to throw together at the last minute on a shoe string budget is a trip into the Boundary waters for 3 or 4 days. It only costs about $25 to get an entry pass and you can stay as long as you want. It is a real backpacking adventure as you must pack light or the portages will wear you out. We take a butane stove that we can boil water with for our coffee, oatmeal, dehydrated dinners. Since cans and bottles are not allowed in the Boundary Waters Canoe Area Wilderness (BWCA) we take some foil packs of creamy noodle entrees with the hopes that we can boil a fresh fish into them as well. I take a foil pack of salmon or two in case the fish are not cooperating. Because I have a teenage son with a high metabolism, I take an ample supply of dried fruit, granola and skittles and powdered energy drink mix. We filter our water with a small backpacking water filter right out of the lake into our water bottles. I habitually take too much fishing gear and need to get better about lightening the load there. A warm sleeping bag is necessary as it sometimes gets below 40 at night. We take a small rain fly and some rope to help us hang out in camp on rainy days. We usually pack all the gear into a waterproof backpack and tie it to the canoe and run some ropes across it just in case we tip the canoe. I have never accidently tipped a canoe but I have certainly seen others do it especially in rivers where the current and log jams can be very treacherous.

If you tip your canoe in a river, swim to a muddy bank and climb out. Do not swim to a fallen log as the current might sweep you under the log which would be very dangerous. Keeping your center of gravity low in the canoe by kneeling with your knees against the sides is your best defense against tipping the canoe in heavy waves or current.

You can rent a lightweight Kevlar canoe from one of the many outfitters for 35 to 40 dollars a day. They weigh in at 40 pounds which is much lighter than my 62 pound Royalex canoe. Ideally, you would want one man to carry the canoe while the other man carries the backpack on portages. I usually end up carrying more than the canoe and we usually make two trips at every portage. We like to make a base camp and then make smaller day trips to different lakes for fishing then return to the base camp. After doing that for a few years, I am contemplating packing light and doing more paddling and portaging now that I have a faster and lighter canoe.

I have been hiking around the neighborhood with a 36 pound back pack trying to get my back, shoulders and neck and trapezius muscles in shape for portaging and backpacking. I have found that I need to slow my pace and keep my knee bent as I place my front foot or my knee starts complaining a little bit. I have learned to not strain my neck against the weight of a heavy pack as that can lead to a serious neck ache and headache.

Imagine setting up camp on a lake lined with five different kinds of spruce and fir trees and not a single building in sight. You might see another canoe party go down the lake once a day but other than that, you have the entire lake all to yourself except for the loons and eagles and beavers. It takes a little getting used to having nothing to do but paddle, fish, portage and camp. In our civilized world of many distractions and sensory overload, it can be hard to unwind and learn to relax doing nothing but relaxing in camp or in the canoe.

Each lake can be so different up there. Most are crystal clear and cold. Some are tea-stained and heavy with vegetation. The fish grow slowly in the cold water. The animals in the BWCA are not as numerous as in Iowa. They have less to eat in the pine forests compared to the oak and hickory forests of Iowa. Not to mention the ocean of corn and soybeans in Iowa as well. But the solitude and scenery you can find in the BWCA is breathtaking. It is quite possible to see a moose in some of the lakes with more vegetation. On some of the lakes you might have to portage over a beaver dam when traveling through a narrow area.

We really like to catch a few fish and make a shore lunch at one of the many National Forest Service campgrounds in the BWCA. Some of my fondest memories when I was a kid were of shore lunches with fresh fish in Minnesota. We had a Native American guide once that filleted my northern pike with a pocket knife on the shore of the lake and then he put it back in the water and we watched it slowly swim away down into the lake with no sides.

There are bears so you need to hang your food and trash in a bear bag from a tree. They allow you to take a firearm for protection into the BWCA. Although you probably will never need it, a gun can be comforting when you are miles and days away from any sort of help. I am not so much afraid of the bears as I am my wife if I ever let anything happen to my kids while I was up there so I usually carry a revolver. A big can of pepper spray for bears would probably be more effective than a firearm.

You can find out more about the BWCA by visiting their website at www.bwca.com, www.bwcaw.com or my favorite, www.sawbill.com . Sawbill Outfitters is located in a National Forest Service campground where you can get unlimited day passes into the BW. They are at the end of a 25 mile road into the National Forest. They are a three generation family run business. They still do not have electricity or phone service. They have their own generators for electricity and satellite phones. They can help you get outfitted partially or completely and they have reasonable rates. Having the National Forest Campground right there is very convenient also. Many people simply stay in the campground and go out for day trips to the closer lakes.

September

September turns the corner from summer to fall in my prairie garden. The asters of fall are starting to make their grand entrance. Who would not thrill to see a dozen Monarch butterflies gathered on a New England Aster with its myriad of purple and gold centered blooms? I have Stiff Goldenrod in my garden but I try to weed out the Common Goldenrod. The annual migration of the Monarch butterflies depends on the massive colonies of Common Goldenrod out in the farm fields. Without them blooming yellow-gold at the same time as the Monarch migration, the butterflies would have trouble getting the energy to fly to Mexico every year.

Fall is my favorite time of year and September holds a lot of opportunities to get out and enjoy the outdoors for a hunter. The first hunting opportunities are squirrel season and teal season.

Kids are taught to hunt by going squirrel hunting. Being able to sit still long enough for a squirrel to come close or spotting a far off squirrel and being able to walk close enough for a shot are fundamental skills.   In the early season, shagbark hickory nuts are the earliest ripening nuts. The squirrels race across the treetops to the shagbark trees and then feast on the new nutcrop. They end up biting off the ends of the twigs and dropping a lot of leaf clumps down from the heights where they eat the hickory nuts. I enjoy watching their aerial acrobatics as they take death defying leaps from one branch to another 80 feet above the forest floor. Squirrels will run over the fallen logs on the forest floor. I think running on the logs gives them a couple advantages. One they can see more when up on the logs and two, it is quieter than running through the leaves.

I was taught to squirrel hunt by sitting on a hillside with a good view of the forest, preferably with a good view of some fallen trees and just sitting there waiting for the squirrels to move close by. You can move every 45 minutes or so to another sitting location, still hunting as you move. This is when knowing which trees are the oaks and which are the hickories comes in handy.

Later in the year you might see the squirrels chasing each other up and down and around the tree trunks. Usually, I think they are just siblings playing ring around the rosy. Sometimes however, you can tell that one is more aggressive and the chase is more of a battle over territory. Squirrels have a lot of muscle and energy from the nuts that they eat.

30

One time we were building duck blinds on the Mississippi river during the opening day of squirrel season and we were invited to lunch by some men that lived on the river. They lived in a house raised up on poles and they made their living by commercial fishing with hoop nets. Well, when we arrived for lunch, there was a big pot of white gravy on the stove. When it came time to eat, they gave me a piece of bread then ladled out a whole squirrel onto the bread. The squirrel still had it's paws and whiskers on. I asked why they did not cut the heads off their squirrels and they said they eat the brains too. So, now when I watch the reality shows with the city people trying to survive in the wilderness, I laugh at them complaining about how hungry they are when they do not eat the heads of the animals they have shot.

One of my fondest memories was the last retrieve of my childhood dog. Poky was a big black lab with a lot of hunting experience. Her hips became arthritic and she could not hunt much anymore. She and I were on a point of land near a giant pin oak tree when I dropped a passing blue winged teal. She waded slowly into the water and swam out and retrieved the duck for me. She sat down and smiled up at me as I took the duck from her. I gave her a hug and cried a little when she retrieved the duck for me knowing that her life was slipping away and that this was a special moment. Did you know that dogs can smile? Dogs can cry also from missing someone but that is not as fond a memory...

I took care of the dogs every day. I cleaned their kennel, fed them and took them for a run in the woods. I saw Poky do some amazing retrieves. Once she had to break through about 70 yard of ice to get a duck. She would start to climb up on the ice then it would break and she would fall into the cold water all the way out to that duck. I was worried for her. I saw her get stuck in a snowdrift once trying to get up out of a ditch and our younger male German Shorthaired-pointer, put his head behind her hips and pushed her up the bank through the snowdrift.

They were just hunting dogs to my father. They did not get the love that most dogs get as they were rarely ever allowed into the house. Once they could not hunt anymore, he would get rid of them. But, our dogs always loved us. Dogs are unique in that they are the only animals that love you more than they love themselves. I know dogs are not created in God's image like humans but I still believe they will be in heaven because I asked God for my dogs to be there.

During September in Iowa they have a youth deer hunting season for kids under 16 years old that runs for three weekends. If the kids do not get their deer during that time, they can use that youth tag during any of the other deer seasons. The kids do not need to have passed the hunter safety class, they just need to be accompanied by a licensed hunter. I enjoy taking kids hunting during the youth season. It is warm and the deer are easy to get close to. We spend time at the range getting firearms instruction and knowledge about where to shoot a deer for a quick kill. I try to take the kids out scouting in the winter and early spring before the season to show them there is more to hunting than merely shooting a deer. I basically take the kid out, show him where to sit so that all he has to do is raise his gun and shoot the deer.

I was sitting behind a fallen log with a kid from my son's boy-scout troop once. That kid is now an eagle scout and I hope he can go with us to Philmont next year. A nice little six point buck came down the trail about 20 minutes into our first day. Ordinarily, I would pass on a small buck like that but it was very close and an easy shot so, for a first deer, hunting public land, we made an exception. He was using my scoped Remington 870 12 gauge. He was resting it on the fallen log and the deer was no more than 15 yards away. He made a good shot and the deer dropped right away. Later he confided that he was glad to be resting the gun on the log because he was shaking quite a bit at the time. Adrenaline causes you to shake like that.

My son's first deer also came during the youth deer season. We actually saw that same deer the year before and did not get a shot. We had to hunt all three weekends and finally got that deer, a big bodied nine pointer on the last day of the youth season. I believe that God is in charge of deer and bullets. God has taught my son patience and perseverance by not making it easy on him. My son has to work for what he achieves; it seldom comes easy for him. I respect him for his perseverance and positive attitude. He was proud of that deer as I was of him. He had been shooting BB guns and pellet guns and airsoft guns his whole life it seems so he has become a very good rifleman.

For proficiency with a rifle, besides having a good solid rest, it is all about the trigger pull. You need to tighten up and squeeze off the trigger while holding your breath and between heart beats without flinching. Breathing imparts movement to the gun barrel, so you have to take a deep breath and hold it to minimize that movement. If you cross your legs and relax the top one, you will notice that it moves with the pulse rate of your heartbeat. The same thing happens with your gun barrel. It moves to the pulse of your heartbeat in your arms. One of the best ways to not flinch is to keep your eyes open and do not blink when the gun goes off. You need to concentrate and slowly pull the trigger instead of jerking it. You want to maintain the sight picture without blinking as the hammer falls and the gun goes off so that you do not flinch. If you hurry the shot and close your eyes in anticipation of the recoil from the gun going off, your shot will not be as accurate.

Shooting a pistol is a different story. You need to have a solid stance, like a front stance or a horse stance in martial arts. You need to extend both arms straight and hold the pistol/revolver firmly like you are gripping a hammer. Your non trigger hand should wrap around your trigger hand with both thumbs pointing forward. No thumbs under the back of the slide please! Keep your trigger finger pointed straight ahead on the side of the gun and not in the trigger guard until you are ready to shoot. I pull the trigger straight back with the first pad of my finger instead of the joint. When I use the joint of the finger on the trigger, I tend to squeeze my hand more and impart a downward motion on the barrel as my hand tightens up. Pulling straight back with the pad of the finger lets me maintain a good sight picture so that I do not flinch when the hammer falls. Again accuracy with a pistol is mostly about the trigger pull. Something different about pistol shooting is that you should concentrate on the front sight intensely. Concentrating on the top of the front sight and centering it in the rear sight is an important part of pistol shooting. You can line up the top of the sight on the bottom of the bulls eye using your peripheral vision but you should not shift your depth perception from the front sight to the target and back again.

Shooting a shotgun is all about timing and follow through. You should use a horse riding stance or have your lead foot slightly ahead to support the weight of the barrel. Your knees should be bent, almost in the start of a squat position as that puts more counterweight further back so you can swivel freely at the hips. When they throw the clay bird you should keep both eyes open and move the gun up into your sight picture while watching the bird. You track the bird with the gun swinging through from behind it and pulling the trigger as you swing through it. You need to concentrate on the bird and use your peripheral vision to notice when the bead is lined up with the bird. It is important to concentrate on the swinging motion and keep the swing going. If you change your focus from the bird to the bead then back again you will tend to stop swinging as you pull the trigger. You need to follow through and pull the trigger as you swing through the bird in order to lead the bird and shoot where the bird is flying. If you stop swinging you will shoot behind the bird. Now if the bird is going straight away, swinging side to side is not as important. It is more important to pull the trigger as the bird reaches the apex of its flight and hangs in the air before it starts to fall. If you wait to pull the trigger after the bird has started to fall, you will probably end up shooting over the bird.

Shooting a bow is again all about the release. The most common mistake is to not follow through. If you do not concentrate on releasing the arrow and not moving your head or bow hand then you will impart some movement to your bow and that will throw off your arrow. Most archers use a release that clamps the string and has a trigger to release the clamp. They usually have a loop tied to the bowstring around the nocking area. That type of release eliminates the twisting of the bowstring we used to get from drawing and releasing the string with just our fingers. It is just as important to keep your sight picture and not flinch when you release the string on a bow as it is when you pull the trigger on a rifle. Additionally, the bow hand holding the handle of the bow should not squeeze the bow too tightly as that can torque the bow and cause the arrow to change direction as it leaves the bow.

October

I enjoy seeing the last asters of the season in October. Small white blossoms on Meadow and Frost asters will still be blooming after it turns cold. Along the trails in the woods I see a light blue aster only about 2 feet tall. October is the month to visit some of my favorite prairies and collect some seeds that I can sow into my own prairie in the spring. I enjoy finding Bergamot plants in the wild after they are done blooming and crushing their heads and leaves between my fingers to smell their fragrance. I have never made tea from them but it can be done. I like showing kids how the stems of the bergamot are square on the bottom of the stem and feeling the 4 sides. October in Iowa is really a special time. The harvest is in full swing. The trees are changing color. The days are warm and the nights are cool. I spend a lot of time in the woods in October.

I can remember hunting for geese on the Mississippi river when I was young from a pontoon blind anchored in the middle of the river. You could park two 18 foot jon-boats in the blind. They had a gas stove in there and we made lunch while listening to the world-series on the radio. They had hundreds of goose decoys around the blind. We did not see much that day. We had two Canadian geese come down the river and land at the edge of the decoys about 70 yards away from the blind. We shot at them and wounded one. They flew to the Illinois side of the river and the wounded one was shot by another blind full of hunters. Then I witnessed something that makes me not want to hunt Canadian geese anymore. The other goose flew in circles around that blind calling for his mate that had been shot until it was finally shot as well. Knowing that Canadian geese mate for life and after watching that, I have not wanted to shoot another Canadian goose since. I do not have the same sentimentality for philandering ducks however.

One time I watched a red tail hawk hopping from one small tree to another through the forest. As he came closer, I could see that he was chasing a little black mink through the woods. At first I thought the mink was about to die and I feared for his life. But, as they passed me and moved away into the forest it became clear that the hawk could get the mink at anytime but he was just chasing him through the woods for fun or curiosity. The mink did not know it was a game and was running with determination as if his life depended on it.

Another time, we were sitting behind a fallen tree and two noisy woodpeckers were making all kinds of racket around us. Then all of a sudden about 10 feet over our heads, a Coopers hawk dove down and tried to grab one of the woodpeckers out of the air. We could see the hawk as it upended itself with talons outstretched and tried to grab the woodpecker. Well that shut them up anyway. They laid low after that near death experience.

I was in the woods one beautiful October day when two deer came to within about 35 yards of my stand. They stood there for quite a while each looking over each others hind quarters. All of a sudden the woods exploded as two coyotes charged in on the deer from two separate directions. The deer rocketed out of there in separate directions. Evidently the deer were alerted to the presence of the coyotes and were covering each other's blind spot for the first indication of danger. After the deer had vaporized, the coyotes ended up directly under my tree. The big male had a snarl on his lip and the hair on his neck was standing up and he scratched the leaves with a few aggressive scratches then pretty soon they both loped off after the deer in separate directions. Does that paint a picture of what life is like in the woods for you? Coyotes run all night long. They have amazing endurance but they are no match for the bullet like speed of the whitetail deer.

I can remember sitting in a tree-stand during early muzzleloader season during a thunderstorm. I know, being in a tree during a lightning storm is not a good idea. I was at the end of a cornfield, just into the woods and there were staghorn sumac trees around the edge of the corn field glowing red in their fall colors. As it started to rain then let up, I remember saying to myself the worst must be over about three times but each time it started to rain harder than before. It really let loose and the only thing dry on me was the percussion cap on my muzzleloader. After the rain finally ended, the light was the most amazing wavelength. It was really quite unusual and made the wet fall landscape look especially beautiful. Then, a nice fat eight point buck appeared under my tree-stand. I lined up the shot and pulled the trigger and nothing happened. I had pulled the set trigger! I lined it up again and pulled the hair trigger this time and the .54 caliber muzzleloader went off in a giant cloud of smoke. The deer ran on crazy legs about 15 feet and crashed into a thorn bush and I thanked God for the deer. It was a heavy deer and a lot of work to drag him out even though I had only a short way to go on level ground.

Something very unusual happened to me once during early muzzleloader season. I was taking an older friend hunting. He was off the bottle at this time but a couple years later died from his alcoholism. It was very foggy that morning. The fog was so thick that we could only drive about 25 miles an hour and even that was probably too fast. When we arrived at the farm, I had to walk diagonally across a large weedy, grass field to the far corner where my ground stand was. I literally could not see the ground it was so foggy. So, I walked slowly and had to feel every footstep to be sure I was not stepping into a hole. This was taking forever so I determined that I would walk faster and have faith that I would not step into a hole. When I decided this, I also thought to myself, this is how much God has been supporting me in my life. Even though I can not see where my life has been going, God has been there every single step of the way supporting me so that I would not fall into harms way. As I had that thought, in about the time it takes to extend your foot and then step on it, the whole field became light. I could see to the fence and tree line on the other side of the field. Then, as soon as it had happened, it became dark again. I stood there stunned for a moment. I wondered if there had been a lightning strike to cause the light. But I had not heard any thunder all morning and, even if it had been lightning, the fog was so thick that I would not have been able to see anything. Wow, I took the experience to be God's way of confirming my thought that He has been there supporting every little step in my life, keeping me from harm. To this day I still marvel at the awesome power of God that is more immediate and more accessible than we realize. I asked God in prayer what the experience meant and the Holy Spirit inside me confirmed my thoughts that this was God's way of confirming how much he has been providing for me and keeping me from harm.

The first time I ever felt the Holy Spirit inside of me was kind of surprising to me. I was driving at the time, not really paying attention when I felt the Holy Spirit leap inside me. It happened at the same time as the words of Jesus were being broadcast on the radio program in my truck. Since then, I have felt this same feeling when I am wrestling in prayer over an important decision or situation. The Holy Spirit confirms that God is in control of the decision or situation. I have seen the decision or situation which was verified by God's Holy Spirit to work out for the best. Other times I have felt the Holy Spirit leap inside me during worship services when I confirm with my heart that, yes, God is worthy of praise. If I just sing along and do not shout out in prayer my affirmation that God is worthy of praise then I never feel the Holy Spirit leap inside me.

I am a tracker. I track animals in the woods and can ascertain how they operate and where they live. I have also tracked the Holy Spirit in my life and have determined that there is good reason as to why the Bible refers to the Holy Spirit as the Counselor. The Holy Spirit counsels us in our decisions and our knowledge of Jesus, confirming what is true spiritually.

I realize many people do not comprehend God or the Holy Spirit. It is really quite simple. If you believe with your whole heart that Jesus was God's son sent to earth to pay the penalty for your sin, then your sins will be forgiven and you can enter into a spiritual relationship with God. A relationship with God similar to what Adam and Eve had in the Garden of Eden before sin entered the world and separated us from a perfectly holy God that can not tolerate any sin. The Holy Spirit is a down-payment on heaven, given to us after we believe and our sins are forgiven. That's what they mean by being born again. Born again means to be born spiritually through your faith in Jesus similar to how you were born in the flesh when your mother gave birth to you. When you are born again spiritually then you can more fully comprehend spiritual things. They say that salvation and eternal life is free for all who believe and that even your belief is a gift from God. The forgiveness of your sin, a spiritual relationship with the creator of the universe now and eternal life with God in heaven after you die is free to us because Jesus already paid the price. Only Jesus, the only perfectly holy man who ever lived, could pay the cost and make such an atoning sacrifice for our sin.

I hope you will use your time in the Wilderness to think about God and try to comprehend how much God loves you.

November

The Indian grass, Big Bluestem and Little Bluestem have all turned a pretty copper color now after the first frost. The Indian grass is still holding on to it feathery seed heads. The Bluestems have given up most of their seeds to the prevailing winds. I enjoy watching the copper colored grass stems above the snow, blowing in the winter wind. Pheasants flock to the prairie grass fields in the winter, especially the Switchgrass fields as they hold up well against the winter snow and provide them some cover to get down below the snow into their own little snow caves.

I remember hunting pheasants after a blizzard once. We jumped about 150 pheasants off the wind-blown, barren hilltop of a soybean field then followed them to where they flew. I would find a hole in the two foot thick snow where a bird had dive bombed in to break through the snow. I would stick my foot down into the hole and move it around to break up the snow and a pheasant would fight its way up out of the snow cave. I was six for six that day. Six shots, six roosters to fill out our two man limit.

During the last week or two of September the deer start rubbing trees and making scrapes. The peak of the rut is around November 7th. It is easier to see a big buck at this time as their mind is on following the does. Did you know that bigger bucks rub their antlers on larger trees? Also, I usually find a large rub at the entrance to a patch of woods.

I think it is like a signpost to the other deer telling them how big of a buck is claiming this territory. Did you know that scrapes on the ground are made under low hanging branches so the bucks can nibble on the branches and leave their scent on the branches?

I am diligent about scent control when deer hunting. I wash my clothes in baking soda then air dry them outside and then store them in a garbage bag filled with leaf litter and acorns and dirt from the forest floor. I spray myself and my boots with scent killer and then attach a scent cloth on my lower leg for a cover scent like doe urine. I once had a 10 point buck come to within a foot of me and smell me before sunup as I sat against a tree. During the rut I will also attach a drag to my boot and drag some doe in heat urine. I have had bucks walk past my stand, hit that scent trail and then turn around and come right back to my stand for a good close shot.

If I ever get sloppy about scent control, I am reminded about how great the deer's sense of smell is. I have had does wind me and absolutely refuse to take another step as they stand still or stamp their foot trying to figure out where I am before they turn around and run off never to be seen again. Once I spook them with human scent, I never see them again. They are very cautious. I don't mind missing them either. If they are smart enough and cautious enough to avoid me, I am glad for them and wish them well. I respect them for their woodsman-ship.

Turkeys can't smell but they have eyes like eagles. My buddy once told me that if a deer sees you in the forest he thinks you are a tree but if a turkey sees a tree in the forest he thinks it is you! That is so true. If you do not move at all, the deer will usually not see you and not be alarmed. However, the slightest movement is usually picked up by a wary turkey from quite a distance and they move out quickly.

In the woods, you should never talk. Whisper if you must but never talk in a regular voice as your regular voice carries a long distance. Also, do not move your head very much. Move your eyes first all over, near and far, side to side, then if it is safe, move your head to a new direction and start scanning with your eyes again.

Out of respect for the animal, never take a shot that is not a sure kill. I always wait for a really close shot where the deer is right under my stand, usually within 20 yards, frequently within 10 yards. Also, I will wait for the deer to turn away from me so it is a quartering away shot. I have shot deer broadside and I much prefer the quartering away shot to guarantee a clean, quick kill.

I scout for deer in the winter a few days after a snow or in March when the snow is all melted and the leaves are all decomposed so you can clearly see the trails. Deer are creatures of habit and very cautious. They will stick to the same trails every year. In the morning, the deer seem to like the ridges or trails just off the ridge to the leeward side of the prevailing wind. Trails just off the ridge like that give them good visibility down the hill and good scent across the ridge from the wind. Of course warming air in the morning brings scent up the hill to the deer on the ridge also. I frequently find a main trail that the does and yearlings seem to stick closely to and another fainter trail to the side of it moving roughly parallel, sometime intersecting the main trail. This fainter trail is more of a buck trail. The secret to deer hunting is finding a funnel area where the geography forces the trails to merge into a narrow area. You need to find the trail where the deer will be during shooting hours. Because deer are nocturnal, the trails you see may be ones they run at night and you will never get a shot at them. Deer beds out in the open are beds they take in the middle of the night to chew their cud. Daytime beds are in the woods or heavy cover usually.

Don't confuse deer in National Parks with normal deer. When deer are not hunted they are not very careful and wary. They become habituated to people. Deer that have encountered hunters are extremely cautious and hard to get close to. One smell of a person and they take off. Does will sometimes hang around stamping their feet and snorting trying to get you to move so they can figure out what or where you are but bucks will just take off.

When I was new to deer hunting, I had hunted all bow season and not shot at a deer. It was the last day of the season, November 30th and I was in a tree stand about 7 feet up in a tree just a couple feet off the trail to the east. The problem was that the wind was also coming out of the east that day because a storm was blowing in. A nice 10 point buck came down and winded his scrape then came straight down the trail which would bring him right by my stand. I had the bow at full draw as he approached my tree. I was waiting for him to walk by me so I could get a good broadside shot. Unfortunately, he got a nose full of me because of that east wind and when he raised his head, he was only a couple feet from my boots. He coiled and shot out of there like a bullet as I let the arrow fly straight and true right through the heart of a tree about 3 feet from my stand! We never did get that broad-head out of that tree.

December

In December you can see great distances through the trees in the forest.   With a coating of snow, visibility and hunting improve. The only colors in the woods come from the red berries on rose bushes and choke cherry trees and maybe some orange bittersweet. You might happen upon a frozen and dried up fall mushroom like the elephant ear. Now is the time to study your tree identification without leaves lessons. Can you tell a shagbark hickory from a white oak by the bark and branch structure? A discarded nut on the forest floor might give you a clue to affirm your guess. The squirrels are starting to hibernate more in their nests. The woodpeckers are active, searching up and down the trunks of trees diligently for very little reward.

We had a memorable hunt on the Mississippi one very cold December day. Three of us were hunting out of a boat blind that day. We had moved the blind into a corner of a pond in the middle of a big island in the middle of the river. I had watched duck funneling down into this area during warmer weather. It was full of smartweed and that floating bright green algae that we called duck weed. It is like flakes of bright green oatmeal floating on the water. It was really cold that day. We were sitting on metal 5 gallon buckets that we had some charcoal burning in to stay warm. They were called Seater Heaters but I called them Butt Burners. It started to snow and then a large flock of big northern mallards started to drop down into out corner of the pond.

They were dropping fast down past the trees when we opened fire. We got 8 birds out of that flock. I was three for three. They were large northern mallards with big and bright orange feet. We packed up and headed for home upriver, more than satisfied with our success.

Most people don't know how to walk in the woods. Man is the only animal that walks on his heels. When walking in the woods, if you touch your toes down first then your heel you will be able to walk much more quietly. If you place your toe down first, that keeps your weight on your back foot so that you can move or re-adjust your front foot position if you feel a stick. When walking on your heels your weight is committed and you can't stop putting weight on your front foot and cracking sticks. If you want to see deer, you should walk very slowly, a couple steps at a time from one tree to another. Then wait at the tree for several minutes scanning all around, especially to new views that have opened up, before you move out to the next big tree. Walk a little and look a lot in order to see animals in the wild.

I can remember shotgun deer seasons from years past. I remember the ones that got away more than the ones I was fortunate enough to harvest. One season, the Iowa DNR actually gave everyone an extra weekend to hunt because the weather was so bad. I was sitting in the woods that morning as it started to sleet. I shot the only deer I had seen all morning, a small buck, just to close out my hunt and get home out of the weather. I field dressed him then dragged him out of the woods. As soon as I dragged him out of the woods and dropped the straps from my shoulders, a giant buck stepped around a row of trees and stared at me at about 45 yards. He spun around and ran off. I was glad to have a deer down and be on my way back home but I laughed at my luck that day.

A few seasons before that I was in a tree stand with a new shotgun with a rifled barrel and a scope. The woods had a 6 inch blanket of snow. I watched as a small herd of about 20 deer came through the woods toward my stand. The big doe that was leading them drew up about 35 yards from my stand. She had smelled my new gun that I had proudly cleaned so well with stinky gun cleaner. She stomped a few times and all the deer behind her started standing sideways and looking around. I knew they were about to bolt back into the forest so I dropped the lead doe, thankful for the meat that she provided.

In Iowa we can not use rifles to shoot deer except in the lower counties during a January antlerless deer season. So shotguns are the main way people harvest deer in Iowa. I refuse to use a smoothbore shotgun with foster slugs on deer. Some guns are probably passable for accuracy but most are inaccurate. The sighting mechanism, a bead on the front is very inaccurate. The slug shot through a smoothbore birdshot barrel does not spin and stabilize enough to make it fly straight. My experience is that the slug comes out like a major league curve ball and you can not depend on it's accuracy at all. Not even at close distances. That is bad for deer hunting. We want to make a good clean kill. In America there is a one-shot kill ethic that has been passed down to us from our homesteading ancestors. They were short on ammunition and long on hunger. You owe it to the animal to make one well placed shot so that you can quickly recover your kill.

I do know some friends of mine that say they can hit a milk jug at 100 yards with a smooth bore shotgun and foster slugs and I have seen the deer they shot to prove it. However, with a rifled barrel and a scope that shoots sabot slugs, it is nothing to hit a pop can at 50 yards with every shot using a good rest, like against a tree. We should use our woodsman-ship and scouting to get close enough to the deer so we can take a good shot. A good shot is good for both us and the deer. Wounding a deer is a real bummer if you do not recover it. If you lose a deer once, you will never want to wound another. Unfortunately many of us must learn from our own mistakes and experience losing a deer once in order to be motivated to never let that happen again. Walking through the woods and taking shots at deer running away from you with inaccurate guns is not the way I prefer to hunt deer. I enjoy hunting from an elevated stand and watching the deer walk by very close and being undetected. That is the true prize in hunting, being able to get close to the deer and go undetected. Then you can be choosy and only harvest a decent sized deer. In Missouri now they have a, 4 points on one side or better law in effect that is turning Missouri into a real trophy hunting state. I wish they had that law in Iowa too as it would promote a little more discretion. I know a lot of hunters on private land that are voluntarily practicing that rule anyway even though it is not law.

There is a saying that a wise man learns from the mistakes of others, a smart man learns from his own mistakes and a fool does not learn from his mistakes but is bound to repeat them. Deer are not foolish and neither should you be.

When I was a younger man we used to live up by West Okoboji lake in Northwest Iowa. We did a lot of ice fishing up there. We usually came back with some jumbo ringed perch and maybe a walleye or northern if we were lucky. I used to keep the little balls from the goldenrod stems when I was pheasant hunting for ice fishing bait. The woody ball that forms on the stem of the common goldenrod, I think it is called a gall, holds the little white larvae of a lightning bug. The lightning bug places its egg into the stem of the goldenrod plant and the stem forms a little woody home for the larvae. If you slice the ball in half you will see the small tunnel and the little white maggot like larvae in the middle of the ball. They make good ice fishing bait for ringed perch.

One time we were fishing a few days after Christmas before the ice had formed across the whole lake. It was only about 2 inches thick where we drilled a hole and set out a tip-up. We baited the tip-up with about a 4 inch chub and we sliced off the top half of his tail. That makes him look like wounded prey to a big northern and elicits a "clean up the wounded" strike from the predator. I think maybe they have been conditioned to know that if a bait fish swims funny, it is wounded and will make an easy, sure catch for dinner. It may also throw a little blood scent in the water when you slice off half of the tail fin. Anyway, we got a hit on the tip-up, let it run for a while then set the hook. Fish tire quickly in the cold water. Good thing too because it was the largest northern pike taken from West Okoboji that year. It was almost 16 pounds and quite fat. It was quite a sight under the glass clear ice as we found out that it would not fit through our 6 inch hole. Someone quickly came to our rescue, drilled a couple more holes and spudded out between them to enlarge the hole. By this time we had quite a crowd gathering around to see the big northern through the ice. It was about this time that the water started coming up through the ice. We were in danger of sending the whole crowd falling through the ice! We quickly shooed everyone back from the hole and landed the fish.

January

There are a couple secrets you should know for enjoying walks in the winter snow. First and foremost would be a pair of really good wool socks. I have a pair of tightly woven merino wool socks that go clear up to my knees. I love those socks. I splurged and bought an expensive pair of long underwear also. They have a wool layer on the outside and a polypropylene layer on the inside against the skin. If I am walking with my quilted, bib-style coveralls on, I would never need the warm long underwear. I have a pair of quilted coveralls that are all one piece also, not just the bibs. Coveralls really lock in your heat so it does not escape around your middle. I picked up a couple of wool sweaters from Goodwill for less than 5 dollars each. They are appropriately named, sweaters. You can minimize the bulkiness of your winter clothes by wearing a wool sweater over a couple layers of shirts. I like a shirt with some big chest pockets for easy access to a cell phone and some cough drops through my coveralls.

Northerner boots are good walking in the Iowa snow where it is mostly flat land. They are green rubber boots that are insulated around the foot. They are not very heavy but have a decent tread design and stand up well to years of walking. They do not have much ankle support however. I have never sprained my ankle in them but most of my walking is on fairly level ground.

The last things you will need to help you enjoy the outdoors during cold weather are a pair of gloves and a stocking hat. For really cold weather I like to use a pair of rag-wool gloves inside my Thinsulate lined elk-skin mittens. I like to go early in the season to my local lumber store and buy the extra large gloves and mittens so that I have enough room to put a liner layer inside. Just a pair of jersey gloves inside really keeps the cold out. The first half hour that you are outdoors in the winter your fingers will get really cold but then they will almost hurt as the blood comes back into them and your fingers will stay warm the rest of the day if you are walking around. If you are not walking, just sitting, you should alternately keep one hand in a coveralls pocket to stay ahead of the cold.

Any tight around the ears and neck stocking hat is good. In really cold weather I love my tightly woven, Thinsulate lined full head type ski mask. If I had ski goggles also to keep the wind off my eyeballs, I would probably be good to 50 below. I have been out in 25 below all day without a ski mask, just a stocking cap and that is not something I would want to do again but it can be done. When it gets to the 25 or 30 below range, I like to boil up a pan of water on the stove to a rolling boil and then run outside and throw it up into the air. It all evaporates with a loud whooshing sound in a big cloud of steam and none of it hits the ground.

The real fun in January comes a few days after a good snow storm. I bought an Outdoor Atlas that shows every gravel road and public area in Iowa and I like to explore new and old areas that I have not been to in a while with my dogs. There is no one else out in January. Hunting seasons are mostly over so you will have the woods to yourself. A few days after a snow, you will see what tracks have been laid down over the past couple days. I remember seeing the first coyote tracks in the 2 mile square section of woods that I like to hunt many years ago. Since then, Mr. Coyote has made a comeback. The habitat around the 2 mile square section of woods has also made a comeback and they are directly related. There is a now impenetrable quarter mile square section of "Tanglewood" that has grown up in a field adjoining the woods. The park staff has planted a nice windbreak hedgerow along the whole north side of the woods also. The hedgerow has an abundance of raspberry vines, gray dogwood, service berry and wild plum. They plant corn fields in the park that they harvest late and do not plow them under until spring. They have done well to establish some tall grass prairie north of the hedgerow down to the lake also. I saw my first covey of quail out there last year. It was in the grass next to the Tanglewood section. Evidently the security afforded by the raspberry vines and plum thickets keeps them safe at night from Mr. Coyote when they are all huddled together into their little sleeping ball. Have you ever seen the 12 inch wide circle in the snow where a small covey of quail has nested for the night?

My dogs do not need a ski mask to enjoy the winter wonderland. Their enthusiasm motivates me to explore the tracks on a sunny winter afternoon. Being able to tell which way the deer were moving in a thick powdery snow sometimes takes a bit of study. I find it interesting how the deer stick to the same trails even when they are covered in a foot of snow. I have seen my dogs smell things through the snow and tunnel down to them so I know that smell emanates up through the snow fairly well. I suppose the deer can smell their trails through the snow also.

February

I enjoy walking along frozen rivers in late winter. Not on the river but alongside it! That is a great way to see the concentrated population of eagles. They concentrate along the rivers wherever there is open water so they can hunt the carp and suckers in the shallow, fast water. They can be seen flying up and down the river in late winter. Take your camera because you can get quite close to many eagles at this time of year.

In late February, if the snow is not too thick, I like to keep an eye out for shed deer antlers. Sometimes I find deer skulls also from wounded deer that eluded the hunters. It is funny how you will find both shed antlers fairly close together. It is always great to find a decent set of shed antlers. It gives you hope that you might see an even bigger set next fall.

If it thaws in late February, the skunks will start to wake up from their hibernation. My dogs are not foolish. They learn from their mistakes. If my older lab smells even a whiff of skunk smell, she stands still figuring it out then changes direction as do I. Hydrogen peroxide and Dawn dishwashing soap and baking soda will take away the skunk smell fairly well. I pray that my younger lab is wise enough to learn from the older labs experience with skunks but I am afraid he will have to make his own mistakes. I try to stay away from river-bottoms in the late winter so as to avoid any skunk lessons.

Late winter is planning time to plan my wildlife habitat restoration projects in the spring. It is amazing to me the variety of life that even a small, 1,000 square foot native prairie grass garden can sustain. The insects, birds, reptiles and small mammals that make a population explosion just because they have a small patch of prairie habitat is amazing. Garter snakes appreciate the insects and mice appreciate the seeds from a prairie. Red Tail hawks appreciate the garter snakes and mice that appreciate the insects and seeds. Rabbits appreciate the warm and secure bedding cover from a prairie. Owls appreciate the rabbits that appreciate the bedding cover.

I just recently purchased 12 acres of land and am planning quite a wildlife restoration project this spring. I ordered some small bare root saplings from the Iowa State Forest Nursery in Ames. I have one songbird packet for $20. It includes the following.

Songbird Packet: 2 Bur Oak, 2 White Pine, 4 Wild Plum, 4 Chokecherry, 4 Gray Dogwood, and 4 Serviceberry.

They sell many other packets for $110. They include the following.

Turkey Packet: 50 Bur Oak, 50 White Oak, 50 Pin Oak, and 50 Gray Dogwood
Pheasant Packet: 50 Red Cedar, 50 Wild Plum, 50

Ninebark, and 50 Gray Dogwood
Quail Packet: 100 Wild Plum and 100 Gray Dogwood

In addition to the songbird packet, I bought a Create Your Own Packet with 50 Ninebark, 50 Gray Dogwood, 50 Norway Spruce and 50 Black Walnut. I also bought 100 Hazelnut bushes for $40. So, for about $160, I will have every deer and turkey in the neighborhood keeping me company and enjoying my hospitality. I will plant some of the hazelnut bushes in the forest at the head of ravines to stop the erosion. I will plant more of them along the forest edge. I am really looking forward to seeing all the animals, deer, turkey and squirrels that the hazelnuts will support on the property. The Ninebark and Gray Dogwood will make good winter food and cover for songbirds and pheasants and turkeys. The Norway spruce will grow quickly to help shelter my feeding area from the wind and provide some winter roosting area. Wind is the enemy of small songbirds in the winter. If the wind gets up under their feathers they can freeze to death. They need to manage their energy levels well in the winter time when food is scarce. The black walnut trees are probably for my great grandchildren's college education. But, until then, they will add variety to my oak and shagbark hickory forest. I also ordered some apple trees and pear trees from the Arbor Day society for about 10 to 12 dollars per tree. I hope they come to me in good shape.

So, all these trees and shrubs in addition to the prairie grass and flower seeds that I harvested last fall, will give me quite a bit of work to do this spring. Once these plants are established, they will come rallying back every year bringing me countless hours of joy watching all the birds and animals that depend on them for food and shelter.

Currently there are a lot of coyotes out there and very few rabbits. It is kind of like playing God deciding who should live and what the balance of power should be when you decide to thin down the coyote population. The Boy Scout camp across the street tried to raise some chickens but they were decimated in short order last year. Most places in Iowa are overrun with raccoons. The raccoon population at the Boy Scout camp is not as heavily concentrated as in other areas of Iowa. The coyotes must be thinning down the raccoon population in addition to the chickens. The nesting success of ground nesting birds such as pheasants and quail and ducks for that matter is inversely proportional to the population of raccoons and skunks. So, if a person decides to shoot a coyote, the ramifications might be more raccoons and skunks and less pheasants and quail. It is a hard tradeoff and not one to be taken lightly. There would certainly be more rabbits if there were less coyotes. Currently there are very few rabbits out at the scout camp and on my farm.

I have always been of the opinion that if you kill it you have to eat it. My son shot a raccoon once and we barbequed it in the crock pot. It came out very tender and tasted good. I never got use to the idea that I was eating a raccoon however as I have seen what they eat. I guess I prefer to eat deer or pheasants or ducks as opposed to raccoons. I have eaten a lot of rabbits and squirrels in my day. Now that it is not so challenging to hunt them, I rarely harvest them. I prefer to merely watch them as I am not really that hungry. I do enjoy helping young hunters harvest some rabbits and squirrels however as it is a big accomplishment for them. Rabbit stew is really quite good. Maybe I will take out a few coyotes in hopes that my new brush piles will yield a few rabbits for me so I can make some hasenpfeffer!

I would urge you to plant a small corner of your yard into a prairie garden just so you can keep your finger on the pulse of the wilderness all around you. May the sun warm your back in the wilderness and peace, pervade your thoughts. God bless you with an abundant life full of peace, joy and the happiness that comes from helping others. Wilderness is best when shared with a friend, the birds and the animals.

Closing

Now, I hope that the wilderness adventures I have described in this book will help to motivate you to get out and enjoy the outdoors. I would urge you to contemplate the wonders of our natural world and get to know the creator God by studying his creation.

Crossing the line of faith and stepping into a relationship with the creator of the universe is the best move you will ever make. Don't be afraid to be honest with God and ask him questions and express yourself to him. He already knows everything about you and loves you more than anyone.

Study the bible with other believers so they can help you understand the symbolism. The Bible is not like a history book or text book. It does have history in it but it has a lot of poetry and metaphors and symbolism. They asked Jesus why he spoke in parables. He answered that he spoke in parables to fulfill the prophecy in Isaiah 6:9, that they would "Be ever hearing, but never understanding; be ever seeing, but never perceiving". You have to read the Bible with eyes of faith and question what God is really trying to tell you in order to perceive the truth. God wants us to stew on and meditate on the meaning of Bible passages so that we can glean the real meaning from it. Salvation is free but it is not cheap. It cost Jesus everything and God wants to give salvation to you if you trust Him and put your faith in Him.

Entering into a spiritual relationship with God will bring about an abundant life full of love, joy, peace, patience, self-control, hope and faith here and now. Your family and loved ones will benefit from your relationship with God. You can pray for anything and God will listen. You can pray for all sorts of things like, your marriage, your kids, your kid's future spouses and careers, your spouse's life, fulfilling God's plans for your life. Many of us want to make the most of our life and we should pray for God to help us do so. You can pray for a strong body so that you can use your strength to help others. I pray that I do not make the wrong decisions and spoil all that God has planned out for me. The mother of Jeffery Johnson, a well-known pastor from Indianapolis used to tell him that he needed to be "prayed up" when troubles came along. You can greatly bless and benefit your loved ones by praying for them so that they are "prayed up" when troubles arise in their lives. Having prayer cover as a youngster is very beneficial. There are a lot of bad choices and bad situations that an adolescent can get into if they are not "prayed up."

I have often wondered why God would listen to the prayers of men. It should be enough to know the Jesus prayed and He commanded us to do the same. I have seen some amazing answers to prayer during my lifetime. Once for example, I was praying consistently for my sister to find a good husband from a good family that would help her experience the good healthy family life that not enough of us enjoy. A couple months after I started praying for her in this way, I had a dream of being in a hedge lined garden. It was very real dream with vivid colors that I still remember. About two years later, I was standing at the opening to a hedge lined garden of a big southern estate as she came down the hill in a horse drawn carriage for her wedding. She married into a wonderful Christian family that is a source of joy to her.

Don't worry about what other people might think if you become a believer. This is just between you and God. If I could tell you only one thing, I would tell you that Jesus is for real and He is all you will ever need.

Made in the USA
Charleston, SC
26 July 2012